McGRAW-HILL
Language Arts

Handwriting

Aa Bb Cc Dd
Ee Ff Gg Hh

McGraw Hill

Grade 3

Macmillan/McGraw-Hill

A Division of The **McGraw·Hill** *Companies*

Published by Macmillan/McGraw-Hill, of McGraw-Hill Education, a division of The McGraw-Hill Companies, Inc.,
Two Penn Plaza, New York, New York 10121.

Printed in the United States of America

ISBN 0-02-244783-0/3
  3 4 5 6 7 8 9 005 06 05 04 03 02

Table of Contents

The Manuscript Alphabet Review

Circle the letters that spell the name of your state.

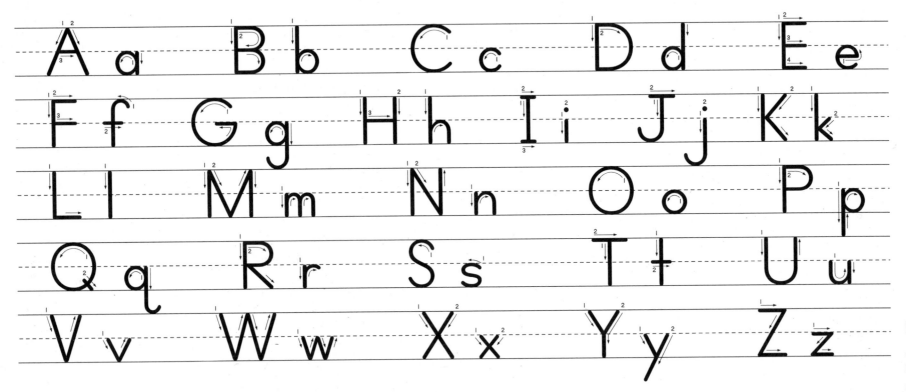

Lines in Letters

Write these letters with straight lines. Then use them to write a word.

E t H F i L I

Write these letters with slant lines.

A y W v k M x

Write these letters with circle lines.

S b D Q o a e

Complete the sentence.

My favorite color is _____.

Circle the letters with slant lines.

Letter and Word Spacing

Space Between Letters
- not too close
- not too far apart
- space of a pencil point between letters

Space Between Words
- not too close
- space of a pencil between words

too close

too far

just right

not like this

like this

Numerals and Punctuation Marks

Trace and write the words and numerals.

1	one	6	six
2	two	7	seven
3	three	8	eight
4	four	9	nine
5	five	10	ten

Trace the punctuation marks.

? ! ? ! ? !   ? ? ! ? ? !

Write this sentence:

My cat has 5 kittens!

Writing Sentences

Write the sentences. Remember to include the correct punctuation.

The world has many endangered

animals. The Asian tiger is one.

The California condor is another.

What can be done to help?

Name _____ Date _____

Signing Up

Fill out the form. Write as neatly as you can.

Sports Club Membership Form

Name: _____

Address: _____

_____

Grade and Class: _____

Interests: _____

_____

_____

© Macmillan/McGraw-Hill

Left-Handed Writers

Sit tall. Place both arms on the table.
Keep your feet flat on the floor.

Slant your paper.

Hold the pencil with your first two fingers
and your thumb.

Cursive Writing Position

© Macmillan/McGraw-Hill

Right-Handed Writers

Sit tall. Place both arms on the table.
Keep your feet flat on the floor.

Slant your paper.

Hold the pencil with your first two fingers
and your thumb.

Cursive Writing Position

© Macmillan/McGraw-Hill

Manuscript to Cursive

Circle the cursive letters that are in your first name.

a a   b b   c c   d d   e e   f f   g g

h h   i i   j j   k k   l l   m m

n n   o o   p p   q q   r r   s s   t t

u u   v v   w w   x x   y y   z z

Look at the word in manuscript. Circle the matching word in cursive.

apply   doggy   apply   oddly

much   nacho   nacho   much

black   black   flash   dark

Circle the cursive letters that begin the names of your favorite characters.

Aa Bb Cc Dd Ee Ff Gg
Hh Ii Jj Kk Ll Mm
Nn Oo Pp Qq Rr Ss
Tt Uu Vv Ww Xx Yy Zz

Write the beginning letters of the months of the year in manuscript and in cursive.

© Macmillan/McGraw-Hill

The Cursive Alphabet

a b c d e f g h i

j k l m n o p q

r s t u v w x y z

A B C D E F G

H I J K L M N

O P Q R S T U

V W X Y Z

Size and Shape
Tall letters touch the top line

Make your writing easy to read.

b   d   l   t

Short letters touch the middle line.

o   a   n   m   c   u   w

These letters go below the bottom line.

g   f   z   j   p   y

Circle the letters that are the right size
and shape and sit on the bottom line.

a   w   xh   n   d   g   p

e   l   b   q   o   f   m   c

© Macmillan/McGraw-Hill

Review

Write the cursive words in manuscript.

journey over towering van

scattered exit quick zip

January February March

Write a word you can write in cursive.

_____

Taking Tests

Write **True** or **False** to answer each question.

_____
----

1. Manuscript and cursive letters all look alike. _____

_____
----

2. In cursive handwriting, letters are connected. _____

_____
----

3. In manuscript handwriting, letters should not be too close. _____

_____
----

4. Names of people begin with lowercase letters. _____

Trace and write each letter. Circle your best cursive and manuscript letter.

Name _____ Date _____

Taking Tests

Complete each sentence. Choose a word from the word bank.

Word Bank					
circle	top	straight	uppercase	slant	middle

1. The manuscript letters t, E, H, L, F, and I have _____ lines.

2. Tall cursive letters touch the _____ line.

3. The manuscript letters Q, D, o, a, and e have _____ lines.

4. Short cursive letters touch the _____ line.

5. The manuscript letters A, M, w, v, and Y have _____ lines.

6. Your first and last names begin with _____ letters.

Strokes that Curve Up

Circle each letter whose beginning stroke curves up.

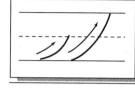 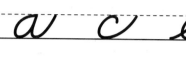 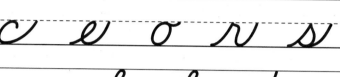 

Trace and write the strokes that curve up.

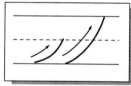

Trace the beginning stroke in each letter. Then write words using the letters.

© Macmillan/McGraw-Hill

i t

Trace and write the letters. Then trace and write the word.

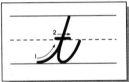 

e l

Trace and write the letters. Then write the words.

 e e e e e e e e

l l l l l l l l

ill lit tie let tile

© Macmillan/McGraw-Hill

Name _____ Date _____

Words to Write

Write the words.

Circle your best words.

tell   title   tie   it

tell title tie it

let tilt lie little

Write a silly title for a book. Use some of the words above.

Name _____ Date _____

Strokes that Curve Down

Circle each letter whose beginning stroke curves down.

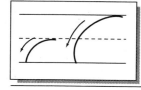

a c e o n s u w I

 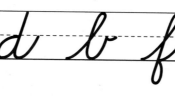 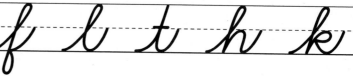

g p q j d b f l t h k

Trace and write strokes that curve down.

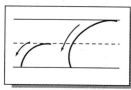
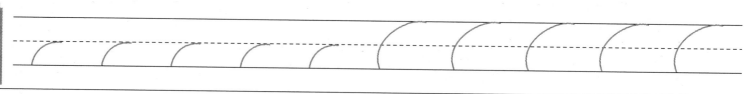

Trace the beginning stroke in each letter.

    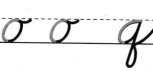 

a a c c d d g g o o q q

Use three of the letters to name an animal. Write the name.

o a

Trace and write the letters. Then write the words.

o   o   o   o   o   o   o   o

a   a   a   a   a   a   a   a

toe toll toil tail ate

tote late oil oat lot

c d

Trace and write the letters. Then write the words and the phrases.

coat   deed   load   code

moon dance   note time

Strokes that Curve Over

Circle each letter whose beginning stroke curves over.

a b c d e f g h i j

k l m n o p w v x y z

Trace and write strokes that curve over.

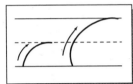

Trace the beginning stroke in each letter.

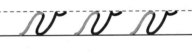

Write words that begin with strokes that curve over.

n m

Trace and write the letters. Then write the words.

n   *n*   *n*   *n*   *n*   *n*   *n*

m   *m*   *m*   *m*   *m*   *m*   *m*

name   *note*   *moat*   *mitten*

tame   *mail*   *melt*   *nine*

Review

Write the strokes that curve up.

Write strokes that curve down.

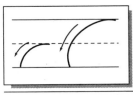

Write strokes that curve over.

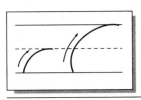

Write slant strokes.

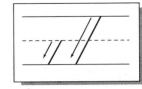

Review

Write the words.

Do your tall letters touch the top line? Do your letters slant correctly?

dime needle meal unite

beetle wombat bobcat

wooden undid fence

bow-wow meow ladle

Name _____ Date _____

Taking Tests

Write phrases in cursive to answer each question.
Choose a phrase from the answer box.

<table>
<tr><td colspan="3" align="center">**Answer Box**</td></tr>
<tr><td>a stroke that curves down
with strokes that curve up</td><td>all the letters
the letters m and n</td><td>the top line</td></tr>
</table>

1. How do the lowercase letters **i** and **t** begin? _____

_____

2. What kind of stroke is at the beginning of lowercase letter **a**? _____

_____

3. Which letters in the word *moon* begin with a stroke that curves over? _____

_____

4. Which letters in the word *list* begin with a stroke that curves up? _____

_____

5. What line do all tall letters touch? _____

_____

Connectives

Trace the connectives.

air tie her met like

an and end in sand

glad just yell zebra games

you zig yarn gap lazy jam

five pick feel quite plan

u w

Trace and write the letters. Then write the words.

u   *u*   *u*   *u*   *u*   *u*   *u*

w   *w*   *w*   *w*   *w*   *w*   *w*

wait wit could would

umm undo uncle lute

© Macmillan/McGraw-Hill

b f

Trace and write the letters. Then write the words and the phrases.

b *b* *b* *b* *b* *b* *b* *b*

f *f* *f* *f* *f* *f* *f* *f*

boat fall bubble off

fine food bat and ball

h k

Trace and write the letters. Then write the words.

h h h h h h h h h

k k k k k k k k k

chick hatch kickball

hook kilt luck kite

g q

Trace and write the letters. Then write the phrases.

g g g g g g g g g

q q q q q q q q q

quacked good and loud

quite a fog

j p

Trace and write the letters. Then write the phrases.

j j j j j j j j j

p p p p p p p p p

pound a beat   pull up

to put on an act

r s

Trace and write the letters. Then write the phrases.

N   *N*   *N*   *N*   *N*   *N*   *N*   *N*   *N*

s   *s*   *s*   *s*   *s*   *s*   *s*   *s*   *s*

pride and joy   set sail

rose blossom   rings a bell

y z

Trace and write the letters. Then write the phrases.

y   y   y   y   y   y   y   y

z   z   z   z   z   z   z   z

zip code   zoom in

pretty yellow azaleas

v x

Trace and write the letters. Then write the phrases.

v   v   v   v   v   v   v   v   v

x   x   x   x   x   x   x   x   x

x marks the spot

vim and vigor

© Macmillan/McGraw-Hill

Review

Trace and write the phrases. Most of the 26 letters are included.

very huge signs on bus

puppy at the end zone

quickly at second exit

are going home with jam

Circle your best letter.

Practice

Trace these connectives. Then write the words.

ball oats van wait boat

bird once very when

cut its day nut can

join yard flash pick

Circle your best joining.

Taking Tests

Write a sentence to answer each question.

1. How do you begin a sentence?

- -

_____

- -

_____

2. What kind of cursive letters begin the months of the year?

- -

_____

- -

_____

3. What is the difference between the cursive uppercase letters **T** and **F**?

- -

_____

- -

_____

Size and Shape

All uppercase letters are tall letters.
Tall letters should touch the top line.

Letters with descenders go below the bottom line.

You can make your writing easy to read.

Look at the letters below. Circle the letters that
are the correct size and shape.

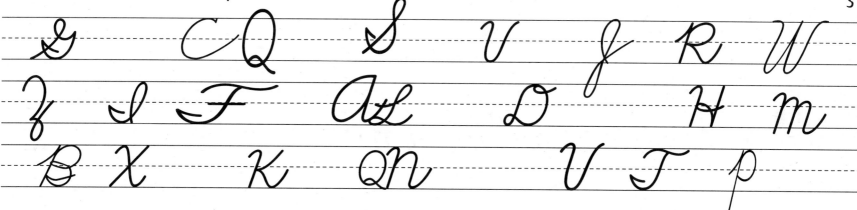

© Macmillan/McGraw-Hill

A O

Trace and write the letters. Then write the sentences.

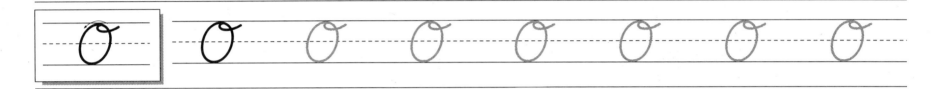

Alice lives in Alaska.

Ollie lives in Oregon.

C E

Trace and write the letters. Then write the sentences.

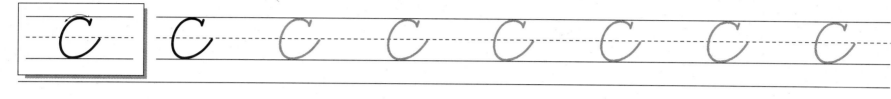

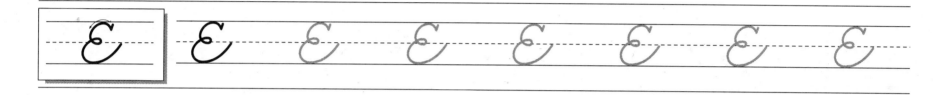

Cecily wants to visit China.

Edward went to England.

Name _____ Date _____

L D

Trace and write the letters. Then write the sentences.

𝓛   𝓛   𝓛   𝓛   𝓛   𝓛   𝓛   𝓛

𝒟   𝒟   𝒟   𝒟   𝒟   𝒟   𝒟   𝒟

Dad asked Dina to dance.

Leo dined at Dina's house.

© Macmillan/McGraw-Hill

46   **Grade 3, Unit 4**

B R

Trace and write the letters. Then write the sentences.

B   B   B   B   B   B   B   B

R   R   R   R   R   R   R   R

Bess bought a Brazilian bird.

Rick can read some Russian.

T F

Trace and write the letters. Then write the sentences.

𝒯 𝒯 𝒯 𝒯 𝒯 𝒯 𝒯 𝒯

ℱ ℱ ℱ ℱ ℱ ℱ ℱ ℱ

Theodore Roosevelt won.

Franklin D. Roosevelt won, too.

S G

Trace and write the letters. Then write the sentences.

 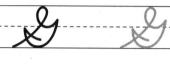  

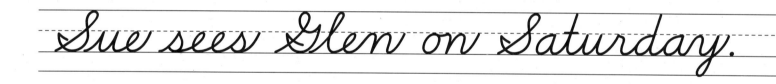

Sue sees Glen on Saturday.

Señora Gomez is the guest.

I J

Trace and write the letters. Then write the sentences.

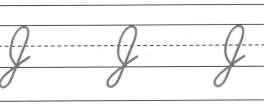

Ida is cooking Indian food.

Jack cooks a Jamaican dish.

Name _____ Date _____

Review
Copy the sentences.

Remember to space letters and words evenly.

Do you know the capitals?

Tallahassee, Florida

Atlanta, Georgia

Salt Lake City, Utah

© Macmillan/McGraw-Hill

Practice

Copy the poster. Write in manuscript. Which writing works best?

Come One, Come All

Gymnastics Tryouts ★ Everyone Welcome

Tuesday at 3:00 ★ in the gym

Trampoline, tumbling, bars, rings

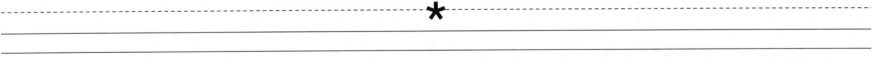

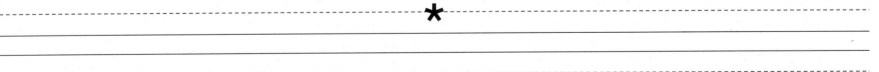

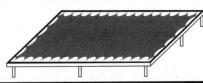

Name _____ Date _____

Taking Tests

Use your best cursive handwriting to fill in the short paragraph that answers the test question. Choose words from the Word Bank.

Test Question: Why is it important to write cursive letters correctly?

© Macmillan/McGraw-Hill

Word Bank

read   send

cursive   words

Correctly written _____

letters are easy to _____ .

They can make _____ *and*

sentences clear. Unclear

words might _____ *the*

wrong message.

Taking Tests

Write an explanation in your best cursive handwriting.

Test Question: Which writing works best when you write a note to a friend? Explain your answer.

I think writing in cursive works best when I write a note because I can write it faster. Cursive writing also makes the note very personal.

Copy the explanation in the box or write your own.

_____

_____

_____

_____

_____

_____

_____

_____

_____

_____

Spacing Letters and Words

You can make your writing easy to read.
Letters should not be too close or too far apart.

These letters are spaced just right.

Draw a slanted line between these words to check that the spacing is as wide as a small o.

Then copy the sentences.

The flowers are in bloom.

Can you smell the flowers?

M N

Trace and write the letters. Then write the sentences.

m m m m m m m m m m m

n n n n n n n n n n n

Minnesota, North Dakota, and

Montana are in the midwest.

H K

Trace and write the letters. Then write the sentences.

 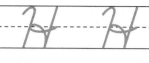   

Hank and Kitty like Hanover.

Kyle lives in Kentucky.

P Q

Trace and write the letters. Then write the words.

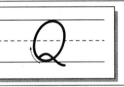

P   P   P   P   P   P   P   P   P   P   P

Q   Q   Q   Q   Q   Q   Q   Q   Q   Q   Q

Quebec   Quin   Quito

Philadelphia, Pennsylvania

V U

Trace and write the letters. Then write the sentences.

$\mathcal{V}$ $\mathcal{V}$ $\mathcal{V}$ $\mathcal{V}$ $\mathcal{V}$ $\mathcal{V}$ $\mathcal{V}$ $\mathcal{V}$ $\mathcal{V}$ $\mathcal{V}$

$\mathcal{U}$ $\mathcal{U}$ $\mathcal{U}$ $\mathcal{U}$ $\mathcal{U}$ $\mathcal{U}$ $\mathcal{U}$ $\mathcal{U}$ $\mathcal{U}$ $\mathcal{U}$

Aunt Violet lives in Vermont.

Uncle Ute lives in Utah.

W X

Trace and write the letters. Then write the words.

_U_ U U U U U U U U U

_X_ X X X X X X X X X

William Washington Wales

X-ray Xavier Xenia X-axis

Y Z

Trace and write the letters. Then write the words.

Y Y Y Y Y Y Y Y Y Y Y Y Y Y

Z Z Z Z Z Z Z Z Z Z Z Z

Yolanda Yukon Yorktown

Zena Zen Zachary Zimbabwe

Name _____ Date _____

Review

Copy the sentences. Circle your best uppercase letter.

The Lincoln Park Zoo is in Chicago, Illinois.

The White House is on Pennsylvania Avenue.

Is there space for a /o/ between words?

© Macmillan/McGraw-Hill

Taking Tests

In a writing test, you are sometimes given a prompt. Here is an example.

Prompt: The letters A and O are alike, but also different. Write a paragraph about how the letters A and O are alike and different.

Complete the paragraph that responds to the writing prompt.

The beginning stroke in both letters curves _____. The letter O, like A, is closed at the _____ line. A, unlike O, is not a round _____. O does not connect to other letters like A does from the _____ line.

Taking Tests

Use your best cursive handwriting to write a paragraph that responds to the writing prompt.

Prompt: The letters P and R are alike, but also different. Write a paragraph about how the letters P and R are alike and different.

Alignment and Margins

All letters should sit on the baseline and stay within the margins.

Four score and seven years ago our fathers brought forth on this continent a new nation.

Copy as much of the sentence as you can within the margins.

Make sure your writing stays within the margins of the paper.

Numerals

Trace and write the numerals. Write the words.

1   2   3   4   5

one   two   three   four   five

6   7   8   9   10

six   seven   eight   nine   ten

Name _____ Date _____

Numerals and Math Symbols

Trace and write the math symbols.

 $+$ $\div$

$\mathcal{S}$ χ

χ $=$

Complete the problems.

$23 + 42 =$ $12 \times 3 =$

$34 + 15 =$ $78 - 25 =$

$56 \text{ dollars} =$

$\mathcal{S} - \mathcal{S} =$ $\chi \div \mathcal{S} =$ $\chi + \mathcal{S} =$ $\mathcal{S} - \mathcal{S} =$ $\chi \div \mathcal{S} =$

Right margin symbols: $\div$ $+$ $\diagup$ $\mathcal{S}$ χ

Left margin symbols: $=$ $\div$ $+$ $\mathcal{S}$

Punctuation

Repeat the patterns in lines 1 and 2.
Then write the sentences with correct punctuation.

???!!???!!?

!?!!?!?!!?

Did you finish the puzzles

What a great idea that is

Yes, run as fast as you can

A Short Story
Copy the story and punctuate it correctly.

Farmer Fred worked all alone One day a peddler came by Look at this he said Wow what an invention What could the farmer do

A News Article

Copy the article on lined paper. Add correct punctuation,
including quotation marks.

Read All About It

*Baytown, May 6 Scientists
have found a fossil of a
dinosaur heart They now
think that some dinosaurs
were mammals This is
amazing news said one
observer*

Name _____ Date _____

Theme Paper

The last four lines on this page are without the dotted control lines.
Paper lined this way is called theme paper.
This is the paper you will use next year.
Copy the sentences.

Many states have state
trees and flowers.
Texas has the pecan tree and
the bluebonnet flower.

Transition to Two Lines

Write the sentences. In the last two rows, write the sentences without the guidelines.

A robin has many feathers.

An ostrich weighs 300 lbs.

Parrots know about 20 words.

Ducks lay eggs.

Practice with Small Letters

This is your first complete lesson without a dotted control line.
Write your letters and words the same way you have been writing them all year.

e u s r a i w m n o

see rain ox run mane

Sam was a curious raccoon.

He came across a fox.

Name _____ Date _____

Practice with Tall Letters

Practice writing tall letters and words with tall letters.
All tall letters should reach the top line.

t   d   l   k   h   b   f

fall   tall   doll   ball   kick

Tiff makes the best pet.

Jill likes to pet him.

© Macmillan/McGraw-Hill

Name _____ Date _____

A Report

Copy the report on lined paper.
Try to keep your letter height and spacing even without the middle line.

The Platypus

Is the platypus a mammal or a

bird? The platypus lays eggs. So do

birds. The platypus has a bill and

webbed feet. But it also has claws.

What do you think it is?

© Macmillan/McGraw-Hill

A Letter

Copy this friendly letter on lined paper.

Make sure the heading, closing, and signature line up.

264 Henry Street
San Francisco, CA 94109
May 3, 2003

Dear Joanna,
    I can't wait to see you! We will
meet you at the airport on
Tuesday. Would you like to go to
the Exploritorium on Thursday?
We can take a picnic lunch.

Your friend,
Maria

Poster

Make a poster to help save Earth.
Write the information.

Plant a tree.
Save Earth!

Join the Plant-a-Tree Club

Contact: (Write your name,
address, and phone number.)

A Form

Pretend you are applying for a library card. Fill in the form.

Name:

Date of Birth:

Address:

Telephone Number:

Your Parents' Names:

Books You Like to Read:

Signature: Date:

Name _____ Date _____

Name _____ Date _____